SEASONS SEASONS SEASONS SEASONS

FALL

Moira Butterfield

Illustrated by Helen James

Smart Apple Media

Published by Smart Apple Media
2140 Howard Drive West, North Mankato, MN 56003

Designed and illustrated by Helen James
Tree illustration page 24 Moira Butterfield

Photographs by Corbis (James L. Amos, KIN CHEUNG/Reuters,
Anna Clopet, John Conrad, Daniel J. Cox, Chinch Gryniewicz;
Ecoscene, Chris Lisle, Craig Tuttle, Larry Williams)

Printed and bound in Thailand

Library of Congress Cataloging-in-Publication Data

Butterfield, Moira.
Fall / by Moira Butterfield.
p. cm. — (Seasons)
Includes index.
ISBN 1-58340-616-6
1. Autumn—Juvenile literature. I. Title.

QB637.7.B88 2005
508.2—dc22   2005042575

First Edition

9 8 7 6 5 4 3 2 1

Contents

All about fall

Fall is a season when leaves change color, the nights grow longer, and the weather is cooler.

The sun gives us life. Without it, there would be no animals or plants on our planet.

Our sun journey

Earth travels around the sun, a huge, fiery ball of burning gas that gives us heat and light. It takes one year for Earth to journey all the way around.

Earth words

The two halves of Earth are called the northern and southern hemispheres. While one has fall, the other has spring. The area around the middle of Earth is called the equator.

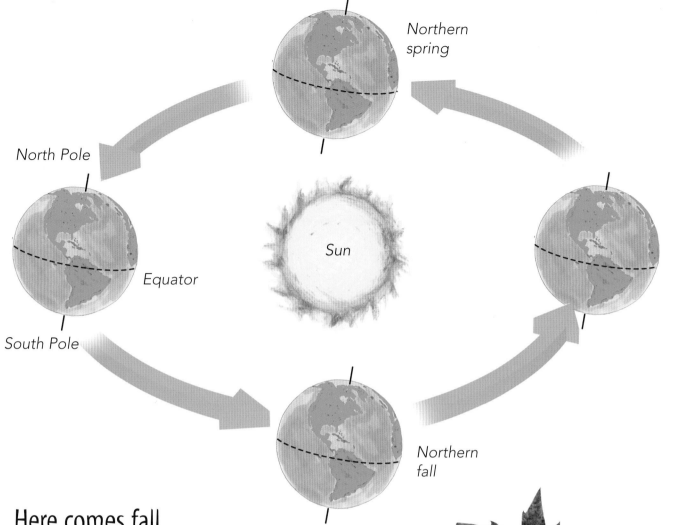

Northern
spring

North Pole

Sun

Equator

South Pole

Northern
fall

Here comes fall

As Earth travels around the sun, the
seasons change. First one half and then
the other half of the planet begins to
tilt toward the sun. Fall arrives for you
when your half of Earth begins to tilt
away from the sun and goes farther
away from its warming rays.

Time for changes

Fall brings lots of changes. The
weather can be very uncertain,
but it gradually grows colder and
colder until winter finally comes.

My fall, your fall

Fall comes at different times around the world. When it is fall where you live, it is spring on the opposite side of the world.

Fall north and south

In Earth's northern half, fall comes in September, October, and November. In Earth's southern half, fall comes in March, April, and May.

In the northern hemisphere, the eastern United States is famous for the beautiful colors of its trees in the fall.

In the southern hemisphere, Antarctica is freezing and windy in the fall.

The equator has wet and dry seasons.

What about the middle?

In countries along the equator, it is hot year-round. There is no spring or fall. Places near the equator have wet and dry seasons instead.

Days and nights

As Earth travels around the sun, it spins in space like a top. It takes 24 hours to spin once. First one side faces the sun, then the other, giving us days and nights. In the fall, the days grow shorter, and the nights grow longer.

Fall light show

In the fall, you can see lights glowing in the night sky over countries in the far northern hemisphere. They are called the Northern Lights or the Aurora Borealis. Natural electricity flashes in the sky, creating the lights.

The colors of the Northern Lights glow and flash in the fall sky over the countries of the far north.

Fall brings darkness

The North and South Poles are in darkness for six months of the year, during the seasons of fall and winter. When fall arrives, the sun disappears from the sky and won't return until spring.

Fall's coming

When fall arrives, the natural world starts changing. Here are some fall signs to look for.

Above your head

As the weather grows cooler, some tree leaves change color and fall off. That's why the season is called fall. It's also called autumn. It's often windy in the fall, and the wind helps to blow the dead leaves off the branches.

Under your feet

On the ground, you might see nuts that drop from trees and bushes. Your feet might crunch over fallen leaves, and you might spot fungi such as mushrooms that grow at this time of year.

Chillier times

You can feel fall coming when the temperature drops outside. We measure temperature with a thermometer that has a colored liquid in it. The liquid squeezes up a thin tube as it grows warmer, and it drops lower in the tube when the air grows colder. Numbers along the tube measure how far up the liquid goes.

These numbers show the temperature, measured in degrees Fahrenheit (°F) or degrees Celsius (°C).

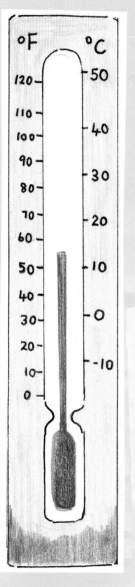

Sunny, windy, or wet?

In the fall, the weather can be very changeable. One day it might be sunny and calm. The next day it could be windy and wet!

Fall weather

Fall can be very windy! It can also be a damp season when you see mist and dew.

Why is it windy?

Wind is air moving around in the sky. Winds blow when warm air rises up and cold air rushes in to fill the space underneath. In the fall, the air becomes cooler, which creates air movement.

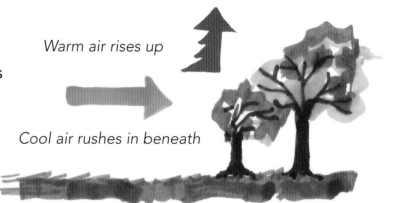

Warm air rises up

Cool air rushes in beneath

Windmills

Wind was once used to power windmills that ground corn into flour. Grinding equipment inside worked when the windmill sails turned.

World's windiest place

Antarctica is the windiest place in the world. Fall is the windiest season there, when hurricanes (very strong winds) blow across the snow.

Power from the wind

Wind is used to turn wind farm propellers. As they spin around, they make electricity.

Foggy days

Fall can be a foggy time. Fog appears when the air cools. Tiny particles of water in the air condense, which means they turn into mist that you can see. Fog is a very thick mist.

Drops of dew hang on a cobweb like tiny diamonds.

Dewy days

When water vapor condenses near the ground, it settles on cold surfaces, such as blades of grass. This is called dew, and it appears early in the morning. It disappears as the day grows warmer.

Fall garden

In the fall, leaves cover the ground, and plants drop seeds, some inside juicy fruits or crunchy nuts.

All about leaves

Trees that lose their leaves in the fall are called deciduous trees. Trees that keep their leaves all year are called evergreen trees. This is why deciduous tree leaves change color and die.

1. Plant leaves take a gas called carbon dioxide from the air and suck up water from the soil. They use sunlight to make these into food.

4. The leaves die and fall off because they are no longer needed for making food. New ones grow again in the spring.

2. Leaves contain chlorophyll, a green substance that absorbs (soaks up) the sunlight the plant needs to make its food.

3. In the fall and winter, plants stop making food. They don't need chlorophyll, so it disappears. That's why leaves change color.

Red, yellow, brown, and orange

Fall leaves can turn different colors even though they are on the same tree. This is because the chemicals inside each leaf change differently. The changes depend on the weather and the sunlight.

Fruits and seeds

Plants make seeds. Sometimes the seeds are surrounded by fruit. Pea pods, berries, and nuts are all fruits with seeds inside. The seeds drop and land in a new spot where they can grow.

All sorts of seeds

Some seeds are shaped like flat wings so they can glide on the wind. Some are hidden inside a tasty fruit or nut to tempt animals to carry them away. Some plants have seed heads that burst open and scatter all the seeds.

A dandelion head has lots of tiny seeds that blow away on the wind.

Fall farm

Fall is a busy time on farms that grow crops. The harvest must be brought in before the weather grows really cold and spoils the plants.

Time to pick grapes

In wine-growing parts of the world, fall is the season for picking ripe grapes from the vines. They are ready to make into wine. In France, this harvest is called the *vendange*. Once all the grapes are picked, the farmers usually celebrate with a special party for all the pickers.

Grapes are picked to make wine and grape juice.

Crops are stored away safely for the winter.

Beating the weather

Farmers must keep an eye on fall weather because they can harvest crops only during dry spells. They often work day and night to bring in the harvest quickly. Some crops are sold. Some are stored in barns to feed animals during the winter.

Secret smelly harvest

Many different crops are harvested in the fall. In southern Italy, it's time to harvest the world's most expensive food, a rare and tasty fungus called the white truffle.

Truffles grow underground in woods. The best places to find them are kept secret. Truffle-hunters use trained pigs or dogs to sniff out where they are buried. They hunt for the truffles at night, when the fungus smells strongest.

A trained truffle pig looks for a rare white truffle.

Animals in the fall

For many animals, fall is the time to prepare for the winter ahead, when it will be cold and hard to find food.

Collecting dinner

The woodland floor is scattered with nuts and seeds at this time of year. Rodents such as squirrels and mice eat as much as they can to fatten up. They also collect food to store in their burrows during the winter.

Getting cozy

Some animals hibernate during the winter, which means they sleep inside a den until spring. Fall is the time to prepare the den.

A badger gets a burrow ready for winter. It takes dry leaves and grass inside to sleep on.

Fat means survival

Many animals go without food when it is hard to find during the winter. They survive by using the fat in their bodies to make energy. They eat as much as they can in the fall to fatten up.

In Antarctica, in the far south, Emperor penguins eat as many fish as they can during the fall to make themselves fat. They have to survive without food through the world's worst winters.

A warm coat

Many furry animals begin to grow a thicker coat in the fall. The extra fur will help keep them warm when winter arrives.

This Arctic fox has grown a thicker coat to keep it warm through the coming winter.

Fall journeys

Many creatures migrate in the fall, which means they make a journey to a new home to find food and better weather. They will return in the spring.

Birds and butterflies

As the sun grows weaker in the fall, more and more animals sense the cold and start moving. The skies fill with birds, butterflies, and dragonflies traveling to their winter homes. Some birds can sleep as they fly on long journeys. Their wings keep flapping as they take short naps.

Underwater journeys

Sea animals make fall journeys, too. Spiny lobsters spend the summer off the coast of Florida. In the fall, they journey to deeper, less stormy waters. Lines of up to 50 lobsters march along the seabed together, each lobster touching the one in front.

Following the food

In the fall, tiny creatures called plankton swim away from the stormy sea surface. They go deeper and move to warmer waters. Shrimp-like animals called krill follow the plankton to eat them. Krill-eating whales follow, too.

The longest trip

A little bird called the Arctic tern makes the longest migration of all. In September, when fall arrives in the Arctic, terns leave the far north and fly all the way around the world to Antarctica. The following June, they fly all the way back again!

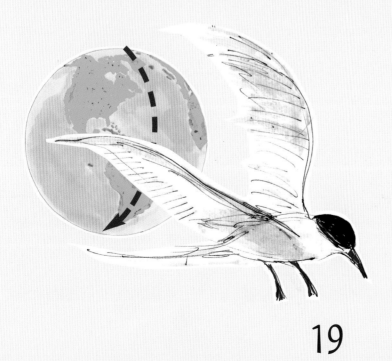

Fall stories

All over the world, people tell stories about fall. Here are two of them.

The moon goddess

This story is told at the Chinese Moon Festival in the fall, held at the time of year when the moon is at its brightest and fullest.

Once, many years ago, 10 suns appeared in the sky. Earth began to burn up and the crops began to die, so the Chinese emperor commanded his best archer to shoot down nine of the suns. The archer was named Hou Yi, and his wife was a beautiful lady named Chang-o.

Hou Yi shot down nine of the suns, and as a reward, he was given a magic pill that would make him live forever.

"Think long and hard before you take this pill. You must prepare yourself," he was told, so he took it home and hid it while he thought about how to prepare himself.

One day, while Hou Yi was away, his wife found the pill and ate it. She instantly flew to the moon, where she still lives in a crystal palace. Her husband visits her at the time of the moon festival, when she is the most beautiful.

Spacecraft lanterns made for the Chinese Moon Festival in Hong Kong.

Anansi and the wind

In the Caribbean, people tell their children many old stories about Anansi the spider-man.

Anansi had a large tree in his garden, and every year he waited excitedly for the fruit to ripen. One year, when the fruit was not yet ripe, the wind came and blew it all off the tree. Anansi shouted at the wind.

"You destroyed my crop. What can I feed my family?" he raged.

"Oops, sorry," said the wind. "Take this magic tablecloth, and when you feel hungry, just say 'Spread, cloth, spread.' It will fill with food."

This worked very well until one day someone in Anansi's house washed the magic tablecloth. After that it didn't work, so Anansi stomped over to where the wind lived and shouted at the wind again.

"This tablecloth is worthless! Do something about it!" he cried.

"That's strange," the wind said, puzzled. "You'd better take this magic cooking pot instead. Say 'Cook, pot, cook,' and it will fill with food."

This worked very well until someone in Anansi's house cleaned the magic cooking pot. It didn't work after that, so Anansi stormed back to the wind's house and tried to boss the wind around.

"You've got to fix this," he ordered.

"Nobody bosses me around like this," the wind muttered, and he decided to teach Anansi a lesson. "Take this magic stick," he said. "Whenever you want something, just say, 'Come on, stick!'"

When Anansi grew hungry, he said, "Come on, stick!", but this time no food appeared. Instead, the stick jumped up and chased him into the river!

Fall parties

Lots of people celebrate fall with parties.
Here are some of them.

Thanks for food

In the U.S., Thanksgiving is celebrated in the fall. People eat a turkey dinner like the pilgrims (the first European settlers) ate after their first harvest. They ate wild turkey with corn, sweet potatoes, nuts, berries, and pumpkins.

Harvest festivals

There are lots of harvest parties around the world in the fall. In European Christian countries, people bring fruit, vegetables, and bread to church to celebrate the harvest. In Ghana, Africa, the Ewe people celebrate their yam harvest with drumming and dancing.

Inuit tug-of-war

In the far north of Canada, the Inuit people celebrate fall with a tug-of-war. They have two teams: the ducks (people born in warm months) and the ptarmigans (people born in cold months). If the ducks win, it is a sign that the coming winter will be mild. If the ptarmigans win, it's a sign that the coming winter is going to be a very cold one.

Spooky Halloween

Halloween falls on October 31 in northern lands. There are lots of superstitions (old beliefs) connected with this night, which people once thought marked the beginning of winter. They thought that spooks and spirits came out on Halloween. People still make jack-o'-lanterns for fun on Halloween night. They once believed the lanterns scared away the spooks.

Paint the fall

Here are some ideas for making fall pictures.

Make your picture glow

Think of the colors of fall leaves and use them in your fall pictures. Try brown, red, orange, and golden yellow. They are called warm colors, because they remind people of fire.

Blow a fall tree

Use a drinking straw to blow paint around and create a glowing autumn tree. You will need a drinking straw, some watery paint, paper, and a paintbrush.

1. Paint a dark-colored trunk using thick, watery paint. Blow some of the paint up from the trunk to make branches.

2. Add different colors, one by one, blowing them around to make a bunch of spiky fall leaves.

Wax and scratch

Here is a way to make a picture of glowing fireworks or a bonfire on a dark fall night. You will need crayons, black poster paint, a sharp-ended paintbrush, and some newspaper.

1. Put the newspaper under your picture, because wax and scratching is quite messy.

2. Cover a piece of paper with thick lines of crayon. Try diagonal red and yellow for fire, or stripes of several colors for fireworks.

3. Cover the entire paper with the poster paint. When it's dry, paint another layer to make it thick.

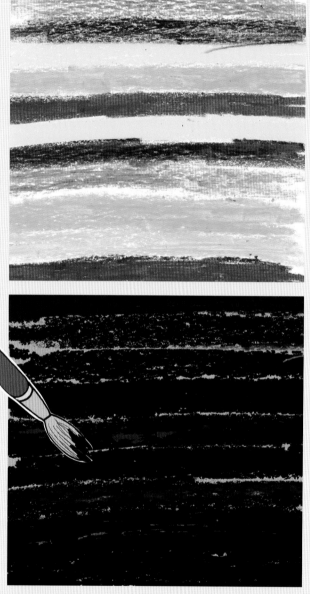

4. When the paint has dried, use the end of your paintbrush to scratch away the paint to show the crayon beneath.

25

Make a piece of fall

Make some wood people puppets from fall leaves, and a mini spinning windmill.

Wood people puppets

Go for a woodland walk on a dry day and take a plastic bag. Collect some dry leaves and twigs. You will also need stiff, thick cardboard, scissors, glue, tape, and markers or paint.

1. Cut out a body shape from the cardboard, as tall as two big leaves.

2. Coat the body with glue. Stick on big leaves to make a skirt, and small ones to make sleeves and hair. Let the puppet dry overnight.

A shape with a wide skirt

3. When the puppet is dry, tape a twig across the back to make arms. Tape a thick stick to the back so you can hold your puppet.

Windmill

To make this wind toy, you will need two squares of sticky-backed paper in two different colors, glue, scissors, a ruler, a strong drinking straw, and a pin.

1. Stick the two pieces of paper back to back so that the edges match.

2. Fold the square diagonally twice to make crease marks in the shape of an X.

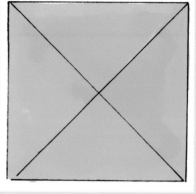

3. Use your ruler to measure and mark halfway along each part of the X. Then cut to the marks from the points of the square.

4. Fold every other point into the middle and glue them down.

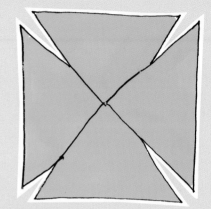

5. Push the pin through the middle and into the top of the straw. Then blow the windmill to make sure it spins!

Be a fall scientist

Discover some fall science by finding out what the wind carries, and the secret of moving air.

Catch things on the wind

You will need a paper plate, some string, some petroleum jelly, scissors, and a magnifying glass.

1. Ask an adult to punch a hole in the paper plate so that you can hang it up with the string.

2. Smear the petroleum jelly over one side of the plate.

3. Hang it outside for an hour or so on a dry, windy day.

4. Bring it in and use your magnifying glass to see what the wind has blown onto your plate. You might find insects, dust, bits of grass, or seeds.

The secret of moving air

Air moves when it warms up. You can prove this by making a spiral mobile. You will need some thick paper, a dinner plate to trace around, a pencil, scissors, and string. Test your mobile over a central-heating radiator.

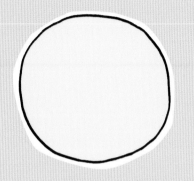

1. Trace around the plate to make a circle on the paper. Draw a spiral inside the circle and decorate it with stripes, or make it look like a wriggly snake.

2. Cut around the circle and the spiral.

3. Ask an adult to help you thread the string through the middle. Pull the paper gently downward so that the spiral stretches out.

4. Hang the spiral high above the top of the radiator. Then watch what happens.

The air above the radiator is warmed. It rises up and makes the spiral spin. Wind is caused by warm air rising up and cold air rushing into the space underneath.

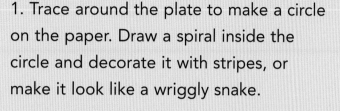

Words to remember

chlorophyll A green substance in leaves. It soaks up sunlight to help plants make food.

crops Plants that farmers grow and harvest.

deciduous tree A tree that loses its leaves in the winter. The leaves change color and begin to die in the fall.

dew Water that comes out of the air and settles on the ground.

evergreen tree A tree that does not lose its leaves in the winter.

fog A thick mist hanging in the air.

fruit A layer that grows around a seed to protect it.

fungi A kind of plant that does not have leaves. Mushrooms and toadstools are fungi. They often grow in the fall.

hemispheres The northern and southern halves of Earth.

migration A seasonal journey that animals make from one home to another to find more food and warmer weather.

Northern Lights Flashing lights that appear in the skies of the far north. They are strong during the fall.

season A time of year that has a particular kind of weather and temperature.

seed A little package containing all the things needed for a new plant to grow.

temperature How hot or cold something is.

thermometer A tube with liquid inside that is used to measure temperature.

water vapor Tiny drops of water floating in the air; the drops are so small that you can't see them.

wind Air moving around.

Index